O[...]

TRADING CRASH

COURSE 2021

VOLUME 3

The Best Guide for Beginners of the Market Psychology to Use the Right Strategies and Avoid the Commons Mistakes to Create Your Passive Income for a Living

By

WILLIAM EARN

Table of Contents

COPYRIGHTS

©Copyright 2020 by William Earn

All rights reserved

This book:

"OPTIONS TRADING CRASH COURSE 2021 volume 3: The Best Guide for Beginners of The Market Psychology to Use the Right Strategies and Avoid the Commons Mistakes to Create Your Passive Income for a Living. "

Written By

William Earn

This document aims to provide precise and reliable details on this subject and the problem under discussion.

The product is marketed on the assumption that no officially approved bookkeeping or publishing house provides other available funds.

Where a legal or qualified guide is required, a person must have the right to participate in the field.

A statement of principle, which is a subcommittee of the American Bar Association, a committee of publishers, and is approved. A copy, reproduction, or distribution of parts of this text, in electronic or written form, is not permitted.

The recording of this document is strictly prohibited. Any retention of this text is only with the written permission of the publisher and all liberties authorized.

The information provided here is correct and reliable, as any lack of attention or other means resulting from the misuse or use of the procedures or instructions contained therein is the total and absolute obligation of the user addressed.

The author is not obliged, directly or indirectly, to assume civil liability for any restoration, damage, or loss resulting from the data collected here. The respective authors retain all copyrights not kept by the publisher.

The information contained herein is solely and universally available for information purposes. The data is presented without a warranty or promise of any kind.

The trademarks used are without approval, and the patent is issued without the trademark owner's permission or protection.

The logos and labels in this book are the property of the owners themselves and are not associated with this text.

TRENDS AND AREAS

Most beginners assume that technical analysis equals indicators. This is not true. Arrows help you decipher what is happening in the market, but they always lag behind the market. After all, it is a derivative of something, and therefore you can never expect an indicator to tell you in advance what will happen. It is simply unrealistic. Instead, it's best to go to the source itself, which appears to be the price chart.

The price chart may seem intimidating, but if we can understand the two fundamental principles by which it works, we can make a lot more sense of it. These two principles are the tendency towards the distance axis and the support and resistance. If you've traded before, you've probably heard of these terms, but I can guarantee you've never learned or used them the way you should.

The fact is, you don't need indicators to trade well. If you can find out the trend against the market reach and the related support and resistance levels, you can trade successfully. It sounds like a big challenge, but it's not as complicated as you might think. The key is to understand the basics of all these terms so that you can work out the reverse price chart.

Let's discuss them one by one.

Trends

The trends on the surface seem simple enough. Every trader wants to understand most of the movement and understand it. After all, this is where price moves in a particular direction, and the more the price moves, the more money you can make.

The problem is that trends tend to run away a lot from beginners. They require decisive votes and, above all, that the trader holds out as long as possible. This means that the ability to pull the trigger on a trade and then have the patience to hold the position until the right time to exit are essential skills. Most beginners lack such skills. The trick in trading trends is to determine how long you want this to take. In other words, if you could find out that the current trend is running out of gasoline, you would know that you should try to get out soon.

The Areas

Intervals are your best friend

The price should be in a range when it moves sideways. If you think sideways, you might think that the price is moving within a well-defined scope, but that is not entirely the case. As you can see in Figure 1, the price seems to be at the same lower-level repeatedly, but at the higher level, the peaks are not quite in tune with each other and reach a much higher high than the others.

This is the thing that makes intervals intimidating for most beginners. The key to resolving this confusion is to realize that the upper and lower boundaries of a gap are zones. You will understand the effects better as you learn about support and resistance. For now, remember that sideways movement up and down doesn't have to have sharp boundaries. Intervals can occur in two places: the first is within a trend, and the second is at the end of a movement. Those that appear at the end of the trends are usually very large and often indicate a redistribution of orders between the two sides of the market. There are always two main sides to the market: the bullish side and the bearish side. The bullish side tries to push prices up, while the bearish side tries to drive prices down.

The tug of war that the two of you are involved in is played on price charts, and this creates a price movement in the way that it does it. At every step of the way, through every single tick on the price chart, the two forces battle each other. Sometimes you are in complete control, while most of the time, the strength is balanced in a specific ratio between the two.

Types of Credit Spreads
Bull put spread

This is an excellent option strategy for beginners. It is a bearish technique where the price of the asset in question falls quite significantly but not jumping big. Two transactions are required at an initial cost. The dealer:

Sold one money bet

They are implemented by buying a lower premium from the money put option and, at the same time selling one into the money put option that has a higher premium. A profit is made when the price of the associated asset is equal to the credit received from the options. The formula for this is:

Reward Received - Commissions Paid = Profit.

A loss occurs if the share price falls below the strike price on or before the expiry date. This is calculated using this formula:

The exercise price for short put - exercise price for long put net premium + commission paid = loss

Break-even formula:

The exercise price for short put - Net premium received = break even.

Bear call spread

This type of option works in a similar way to the above, and the profit depends on the moderate drop in the price of the associated asset. The dealer:

The profit is calculated using this formula:

Received award - commissions paid = profit.

A loss occurs if the share price exceeds the strike price on or before the maturity date. This is calculated using this formula:

Long Call Strike Price - Short Call Strike Price - Net Premium Received + Commissions Paid = Loss

The tie is calculated as follows:

Short call exercise price + net premium received = break even.

This bearish strategy is a little more complicated and is generally not recommended for novice options traders.

Short Butterfly spread

This is a volatility-based strategy typically practiced by medium to advanced options traders. This applies to both call and put options of this type. There are three transactions.

This is not an options trading strategy that a trader should frivolously jump into. This requires careful reflection and reflection. Hence, this is a strategy best used by medium and advanced options traders. However, when done correctly, this strategy offers benefits such as greater flexibility and the ability to profit regardless of the direction of the asset's price. Both the profit and the loss of this type of strategy are limited. This restriction is significant for risk management.

Iron Butterfly spread

This is a neutral strategy with four transactions. The dealer:

- Buy one from the money call.
- Sold 1 to the money call

- Buy 1 with the money you invested.
- Sells 1 to the deposited money

The two calls and puts of this options strategy are the same, and the associated asset and expiration date of all these components are the same. Because of the complexity of this strategy, it is not suitable for beginners. The higher commissions also make it less attractive to most traders. However, the benefits include a higher profit potential. This strategy is useful for making big profits. Hence, with such a large contract, it may be worth pursuing this strategy of increasing commissions.

Debit spread

How debit spreads work?

Unlike a credit spread, where the seller receives cash into their account, debit spreads incur upfront costs instead. The premium is paid from the investor's account upon opening the position and is referred to as a direct debit. This type of strategy is mainly used to offset the costs associated with long option positions. This is because the premium received by extended members is higher than the compensation received by short members. Consequently, the net debt is the highest possible loss value in this type of option strategy. Losses are therefore limited.

Despite this initial cost, debt spreads are generally considered to be safer and less complicated than credit spreads. Debit spreads are therefore used more often than credit spreads by beginners.

Just like with credit spreads, there are at least two options for the transaction. The trader pays for a higher premium option while selling a lower-premium option.

However, just like with credit spreads, the number of trades executed in this strategy can exceed 2.

As with credit spreads, there are call and put versions. The primary call version is set up as follows: the investor:

- Buy one call
- Sell one call (this is the highest strike)

Profit is calculated using this formula:

Size of the two strike prices - premium commissions = profit

The loss is calculated using this formula:

Premium paid + commissions = loss

With the put option, the configuration looks like this:

- Sell one put

- Buy one put (this is the highest strike)

Profit is calculated using this formula:

Size of the two strike prices - premium commissions = profit

The loss is calculated using this formula:

Premium paid + commissions = loss

All these equations are x100 to prepare a contract with 100 shares as an associated asset.

Delta

Knowing the Greeks and what they mean when it comes to options trading can help you become a more educated and effective trader. A more educated trader is the one who is most likely to make a profit. So, let's start with the first Greek called Delta. It is also known as the prevalence rate, but this term is not used very often, and to search for it, one has to find Delta.

The concept behind Delta is quite simple and easy to use. Here's how much the price of an option changes if the underlying stock price changes by one dollar. Consider a delta of 0.68. If the underlying stock changes by a dollar, it means the option price has changed by $ 0.68.

How the Delta changes over time, depending on a few factors. Let's take the money calling option first. When it's in the capital, the Delta rises over time. The reason for this is that the external value decreases while the internal value remains directly proportional to the security price. Hence the Delta will increase. At first, this effect is hardly or not at all noticeable. The less time left for the option, the clearer it becomes. Now let's consider a call option that is out of the money. In this case, Delta will decrease.

For comparison, let's say you have a call option with a strike price of $ 100. Also, let's assume that there are ten days left to expire. If the underlying stock price is $ 99 (so the call option is out of the money), the Delta is $ 0.43. On the other perspective, if the stock price were $ 101 (so the opportunity was in the capital), the Delta would be 0.59.

This shows that when the option goes into the money, all other things being equal, the choice is most affected by the underlying stocks' price. To see how this works, let's move on to this scenario. Under the terms indicated with the share price of $ 101, the call option price is $ 2.54. For example, suppose the stock price rises to 102. Since the Delta is 0.59, we expect that the $ 1 increase in the stock price would increase the option price by $ 0.59 to $ 3.13.

It increases a bit more to $ 3.16, which was a pretty good estimate. When the price changes, the Delta changes too. In this case, it rose to 0.66, which means that another $ 1 hike will significantly impact.

Gamma

Now let' ponder at the next Greek, Gamma. This is a bit darker. Gamma can be seen as a second derivative if you are experienced with calculus. If you have no experience with calculus or want to forget, I apologize for the headache. This means that the range is the rate at which the delta changes if the price of the underlying stock changes by one dollar. As a side note, if you remind from the calculation, a derivative of position over time is velocity or velocity. So, you can think of the Delta as an indication of the rate or speed at which the option price changes.

In this analogy, the range would be the acceleration of the change in the option price. Understanding the details and all the math isn't necessary for most options traders. However, you can follow some basic rules of thumb. The critical point is this. The greater the range, the more responsive the option will be to changes in the underlying shares' price. Another way to see this is to know that Delta changes every time the price of the underlying stock changes. So, the Delta is as good as the value we see in a particular case. With the range, you can estimate how the Delta changes with price movements. The further you are from the exhaust, the greater the range.

The more an option is in the money, the smaller the range becomes. This concludes that Delta will not change that much if the option is in cash for a given change in the price of the underlying security. When the Delta goes to 1.0, the range goes to zero.

Theta

It is a fact that the external value of an option diminishes over time. There is only no getting around it. If an option is further from the expiration date, there is a greater chance that the stock price will fluctuate. This means that fluctuations in the stock price over an extended period could bring an option currently out of the money into the money. As you near the deadline, there are fewer options for it. So, an out-of-the-money opportunity doesn't have that much value as the days go by. Just playing around with a calculator with option prices or looking at them in the markets seems a little puzzling as to how extrinsic value changes. But you can use theta to get an idea of what is going on. Theta gives an estimate of how much the option price will decrease with each passing day. In particular, you will find out how much the option's extrinsic or temporal value is reduced.

Since theta tells you how much the extrinsic value decreases, it is listed as a negative number. Look at an option with an exercise price of $ 50 and a stock price of $ 53. 15 days after expiration, and theta is -0.027 for a call option and -0.026 for a put option. Let's take a look at the call option. The principle is more or less the same for both. This tells us that the 14-day extrinsic value will fall by about $ 0.03. Fifteen days after the expiration, the external cost for the call option is $ 0.29. We, therefore, expect it to drop to $ 0.26 the next day. That's precisely what happens.

The time decrease is exponential and not linear. If an option is in the money, theta will decline in value on the expiration date. When it's out of the capital, it gets bigger. This indicates that an out-of-the-money option quickly depreciates in importance as the expiration date approaches.

An in-the-money option gradually depreciates as the expiration date approaches. For the money, alternatives will increase in value as they expire. With cash options, the foreign value makes up a larger proportion of their price than other options. Although theta will be smaller for the money options, it still represents a higher percentage of the price loss since the outer value is 100% of the total.

In any case, the options will always lose value as the expiration date approaches. Regardless of where your option is to be in the money, money, or money, you can subtract the theta value from the extrinsic value to determine what the next day will be.

Vega

We are now entering a slightly darker area. Vega is related to changes in implied volatility.

If the implied volatility changes by one point, the implied volatility changes the option's extrinsic value. This will be directly proportional to Vega. So, if Vega is 0.42, it would mean that the option price would increase by $ 0.42 if the implied volatility increased by one point. More volatility means higher option prices. The reverse is also true; If implied volatility were to decrease by one point, if Vega were to be 0.42, the option price would reduce by forty-two cents.

So, keep in mind that Vega would tell you how significant implied volatility is on the option price. The higher the Vega value, the greater the critical changes in implied price volatility. Financial advisors suggest that the best time to buy an option is when Vega is below average or typical. If the implied volatility is historically low, it would indicate that the option is a better buy. On the other hand, if the implied volatility is high relative to the historical volatility, it would mean that Vega is above average. This would be a sell signal for the option. But to be honest, most options trading doesn't go that deep into the woods. Make your buying and selling decisions based on whether you are profitable or not.

In practice, it should be considered that if Vega falls accordingly, option prices will fall. When Vega goes up, so does the price of options.

Rho

The last Greek we will see in terms of options is called Rho. This measures the sensitivity of an alternative to changes in interest rates. When you open an options calculator, you will find that it contains what is known as the safe (or "risk-free") interest value. This is the interest rate you would get on the most secure investment possible, usually considered a ten-year US Treasury Department. Generally, when the interest rate increases, call option prices to increase. On the other hand, an increase in the interest rate would mean a decrease in the put options' value. This means that Rho is positive for call options and negative for put options.

Since interest rates only change sharply when the Fed makes a quarterly announcement, it doesn't matter when trading options. Remember that it will take months for interest rates to change (if any), but most options are short-term investments that only last a few weeks. In general, options traders are not going to stand around worrying about Rho these days. The only time that needs to be in the case of a LEAP or a long-term option. Even then, it may not matter as interest rate changes are relatively small these days.

The Rules used in Options Trading

What guidelines must be observed when trading options? What are the Rules? These are essential questions that new traders should be able to answer correctly. We will look at the rules you should follow when trading options. By the end of this topic, you will have the knowledge you need to trade efficiently. These rules are eye-opening for a new aspiring trader, while for an experienced options trader, they serve as a reminder. These rules are not a guide to getting rich, and the rules will help you avoid problems, increase your capital, and make money with options.

Here are some of the rules for options trading:

- Trade short positions.
- When you enter the market, it is obvious to assume the worst.
- It only makes sense to make smaller trades and avoid large trades to reduce the risk of losing a significant portion of your invested money.
- The best advice is to take many small positions because if you only take one large position, you run the risk of being eliminated if you take a loss.
- About 90% of options traders fail because they trade large positions.

- Trading above 5% is considered a great position, and the trader risks damaging their accounts with a bad loss.
- Don't be emotional. The market doesn't care what you think.
- One way to be successful in trading is not to be emotional.
- Don't let your emotions, opinions, or thoughts in the market guide you.
- Have a high number of exchanges. If you know your estimated success rate, you will make a lot of trades—the greater the number of trades, the greater the chances of recovering that expected percentage.
- Options trading is a numbers game and math, and you can pinpoint your chances of success in a particular position.
- You can see your success rate.
- However, this can be why your failure has the same expectations in all your trades.
- The greater the number of commerce, the more constant the success rate will be.

- Balance your wallet.
- You can bet on the price's direction as it rises or falls when you invest in options trading.
- Traders typically focus on increasing the value of the investment.
- However, it would be best if you learned how to offset your portfolio with falling positions.
- Act according to your comfort level.
- If you don't like trading naked options or hedged positions are giving you sleepless nights, then you should act as an opinion speculator and act accordingly.
- Once you are in tune with your strategies, you will find that it is much easier to make money.
- Each strategy is unique and individual and may not work for all traders. This way, you reduce the person's risk.
- Always use a template.

- Failure to verify the option's fair value before selling or buying it is one of the biggest mistakes made by options traders. This can be crucial, especially if you don't have an accurate real-time assessment framework. These are the foundation of strategic investments, and consider the bargains and the amount you are paying for the option.
- Have enough cash in reserve.
- You must have the majority of your cash investment. This can be useful for brokers as they need a margin requirement when trading. You have split a certain amount to cover any losses in your position.
- Try to keep around 50-60% of your investment portfolio in cash.
- Reduce commissions and costs. If you pay commissions and fees to relax and balance your wallet, you could be paralyzed.
- One way to reduce the commission rate is to use cheap ETFs. But for starters, you

shouldn't have to pay any fees to invest in stocks.

Covered Calls are for a long position

To create a covered call, you must own at least 100 shares of an underlying stock. When you make a call, you are offering prospective buyers an opportunity to buy these stocks from you. Of course, the strategy is that you only sell high, but your real goal is to get the revenue stream from the premium.

The reward is a one-time non-refundable fee. If a buyer buys your calling option and pays you the premium, that money is yours. No matter what happens next, you have the money to keep. If the stock does not reach the strike price, the contract expires, and you can create a new call option on the same underlying stock. If the share price exceeds the strike price, the contract buyer will likely exercise his or her right to buy the shares. You will still make money on the exchange, but the risk is that you will give up the potential to make money that could have been made on the exchange.

Write a covered call option with a strike price of $ 67. Let's say the stock climbs to $ 90 per share for some unforeseen reason. The buyer of your call option can buy the stock from you for $ 67. So, you made $ 2 per share. However, you missed the opportunity to sell the stock for $ 35 per share. Instead, the investor who bought the call option from you turns around and sells the shares in the markets at the actual spot price and reaps the benefits. You haven't lost anything, however. You earned the award and sold your shares for a modest profit.

That risk - that the shares will go up at a price much higher than the strike price - is always there, but if you do your homework, you are offering stocks that you don't expect to change significantly in price relative to the duration of your call. Instead, let's say the price only climbs to $ 68. The price has exceeded the exercise price so that the buyer can make use of his option. If so, you are still missing out on a win that you might otherwise have made, but it is a small amount, and we don't take the premium into account.

If the share price does not exceed the exercise price for the term of the contract, you can keep the premium and hold the shares. The price is yours, no matter what.

In the real world, a hidden call is a win-win situation in most situations.

Covered Calls are a Neutral Strategy

A covered call is called a "neutral" strategy. Investors create covered calls for shares in their portfolio that expect to see little movement during the life of the contract. Additionally, investors will benefit from hedged calls on the claims they are expected to hold over the long term. This way, you can make money on the shares during a period when the investor expects the shares to not move much at a price and therefore has no profit potential from the sale.

An example of a covered call

Let's say you own 100 shares of Acme Communications. The price is currently trading at $ 40 per share. Nobody expects the stock to move much in the coming months, but as an investor, you believe Acme Communications has significant long-term growth potential. To make money, you sell a call option on Acme Communications with an exercise price of $ 43. Let's say the premium is $ 0.78, and the call option lasts for three months.

For 100 shares, you will get a total of 0.78 x 100 = $ 78 in the prize. No matter what, you will pocket the $ 78.

Now suppose the stock price drops slightly over the next three months so that it never gets close to the strike price, and at the end of the three-month period, it is trading at $ 39 per share.

The option contract expires and has no value. The buyer of the option contract is left empty-handed. You have a win-win situation. You earned $ 78 more for 100 shares and will continue to own your shares at the end of the contract.

Now suppose the stock acquires some value. Over time it jumps to $ 42 and then $ 42.75, but then drops to $ 41.80 when the option contract expires. In this scenario, you are in a much better position. In this case, the strike price of USD 43 was never reached, so the call option buyer is again left in the dark. On the other hand, you keep the $ 78 premium, and you can still keep the shares. This time the stocks have appreciated; you are much better off than before. So, it is a win for YOU, albeit a sad situation for the poor soul who bought your calling.

Unfortunately, there is another possibility that the share price may exceed the strike price before the contract expires. If so, you need to sell the shares. However, you are still in a position that isn't all that bad. You haven't lost real money, but you've lost a potential profit. You will continue to receive the $ 78 premium plus the gain from the sale of the 100 shares at the strike price of $ 43.

A covered call is almost a risk-free situation as you never lose money even though you miss an opportunity when the stock price goes up. You can minimize this risk by carefully choosing the stocks you use for a covered call option. For example, if you own stock in a pharmaceutical company that claims to announce a cure for cancer in two months, you probably won't want to use those stock for a personal phone call. A company that has long-term prospects but likely won't go anywhere in the coming months is a better choice.

How to Create and Use a Covered Call?

To create a covered call, you must own 100 stocks. While you don't want to risk a title that is likely to take off in the near future, you also don't want to choose a real disaster. There is always someone ready to buy something at the right price. But you want to go with a decent stock so you can earn a decent premium.

You first go online with your brokerage agency and search for stocks online. When you search for stocks online, you can see their "chain of options," which gives you information from a table about the rewards available for retrieving those stocks. You can see them under the offer price. The offer price is per share, but a call contract comprises 100 shares. If your offer price is $ 1.75, you are actually getting $ 1.75 x $ 100 = $ 175.

An important note is that the further away from the expiration date, the higher the premium. A good rule of thumb is to choose between two and three months from the current date. Remember that the longer you go, the greater the risk, as this increases the likelihood that the stock price will exceed the strike price, and you will end up having to sell the stock.

You have an option (no pun intended) with the price you want to calculate. In theory, you can set any price you want. Of course, a buyer has to be willing to pay that price actually to make money. A more sensible strategy is to look at the prices that are currently being asked for call options on that stock. You can do this by checking the asking price for call options on the stock. You can also see the prices that buyers are currently offering by looking at the bid prices. For an immediate sale, you can set your price to an offer price that is already available. If you want to go a little higher, you can place the order and then wait for someone to arrive to purchase your call option at the bargain price.

To sell a covered call, choose to Sell to Open.

Covered Call Risks

Covered calls can pose a risk if you are optimistic about the stock and if your expectations are met, and prices go up. In this case, you've traded the small amount of premium income for a voluntary exercise price limit against the potential uptrend that you could have achieved if you had just held the stock and sold it at the high price.

If the stock price goes down while you're still receiving the reward, the stock is useless unless it recovers over the long term. It would help if you didn't use a call option on stocks that you expect to see a sharp decline in the coming months. If so, instead of writing a covered call, sell the store and take your losses. Alternatively, you can keep holding the stocks to see if they backfire in the long run.

Benefits of Covered Calls

- A covered call is a relatively low-risk option.
- The worst possible scenario is that you have run out of stock but are making a small profit, less profit than you could have made had you not drawn up the sales contract and just sold your stock. However, you also get a prize.
- With a covered call, you can generate income from your wallet in the form of rewards.
- If you are not expecting a short-term stock price movement and wish to hold it for the long term, this is a sensible strategy to generate income without taking a lot of risks.

Limit your Losses and Accumulate your winnings

Every investor experience this at times. You have an outstanding share of your wallet, and it works better every week. And suddenly, there is a turning point, you have hope of recovery, but the decline continues until you get to a point where you can make decisions. If you are not ready to take such a roller coaster ride, be wise. Is your investment doubling? So, sell half of it and secure your investment. When buying a stock, you can work with a stop-loss order. A percentage of 20 percent is typical.

This means an automatic sale when the acceptable loss limit has been exceeded. It limits your losses and allows you to use your new capital to invest in what will hopefully be a more successful business. There is no such thing as a perfect strategy, as you may have to watch the stock recover after selling. A system that will help investors sleep at night.

Show the Overall Financial Picture

Making a profit on an investment is a comfortable feeling. But investments are not alone, on an island or in a vacuum. Investing is part of your overall financial life. Many wealth managers give their clients wise advice: you need to manage accounting as a business.

This may mean that the debt ratio needs to be monitored appropriately. For example, some investors try to counter a smaller investment with a more robust (and often riskier) investment, hoping to make up for a misunderstanding with an absolute jackpot. With this, of course, you are taking an even greater risk, even if it wasn't necessary - an unfortunate side effect for someone who loses sight of their entire accounting. Slowly attempting to resolve this misunderstanding by creating an emergency fund would undoubtedly be a more reliable approach to the problem. This way, you make a sustainable solution and learn from a mistake while correcting it. It is particularly important to have a solid financial foundation before venturing into the stock market. Every other aspect of this personal financial accounting must be perfect.

Build a Buffer for yourself

Investing is never without risk. Risk-free investing doesn't pay off. It only costs money. In order not to jeopardize your healthy financial situation, set aside some money in advance. We usually assume that six months of fixed costs are enough to make up for the worst times. If there are indispensable opportunities in the financial markets, you can still use some of this capital to participate. Consider whether these options are worth your buffer.

Feel Comfortable with your Strategies and Investment

Many people who invest and invest today grew up with a different zeitgeist. Thirty years ago, it was fashionable to get as much return as possible. Thanks to the internet, the decline in pensions and the changes in the banking landscape have changed a lot over time. Modern investments and investments focus mainly on risk and no longer on return. Most people who invest with an additional annuity focus on avoiding losses rather than making big profits. So, your hope is not to get rich or more decadent per se, but to have enough capital in old age to survive.

Investing is not a Hobby

Don't get us wrong - investing can be incredibly fun, but you can't see it as a no-obligation hobby. The big banks see investing as a very competitive activity. This is why it is best to look at your portfolio through the eyes of a professional. It is vital to have a good understanding of your portfolio and to understand where your profits, but also your losses, come from. You also need to be able to understand the companies you are investing in. Once the whole process is done, everything becomes a lot easier. "Is this investment or investment making me money, or am I going to rip it off?" An obvious question is not always asked.

Beginners often invest in stocks that they find attractive - the wrong motivation, often with the false result. In the beginning, investing can sometimes be very similar to gambling, and many beginners want to understand how the stock market works. You will soon see the movements of major indices, but the real work doesn't begin until you take investing seriously. Benjamin Graham said it a few decades ago: "Only make smart investments if you see it as a business." Fund managers, analysts, traders, and other experts in financial centers take stock trading very seriously and are therefore better off taking the challenge.

Not Consider the Stock Exchange as a Casino

Anyone who plays poker knows that "all-in" already dare to pay everything. Put all your money into one game in hopes of surviving or winning the jackpot. Don't rely on this opportunity when you talk about the stock market. Betting all your money on a single stock is never a good idea. Even the most experienced stock traders diversify their portfolios to minimize losses. There have been a lot of exciting IPOs recently. Although the attraction for investors and investors is very high, most of them are aware that this is not the best choice. Beginners are often blinded by the atmosphere, applause, and influence of others. Therefore, always make sure that you are not playing for money. You invest it for a specific purpose.

Financial Resources

Before you start investing, you should be better informed about economic developments and the prospects, markets, and stocks that interest you. You don't have to look far: read the newspaper every day. Financial journals like De Tijd, Financial Times, and Wall Street Journal can help you keep up with the topics that matter most. You can also visit financial websites like Yahoo Finance. Professional investors also use accounts for services like Bloomberg and Reuters. Since everyone is learning the same things at the same time, these may not be the places where the distinction can be made. Still, don't try too hard to follow in the footsteps of the experts. Some of the most famous investors, such as Peter Lynch, have suggested that clues from everyday life might provide more inspiration.

Build a Strategic Model

For example, Lynch "used" his wife's shopping habits to analyze which brands have gained popularity. According to Lynch, traders and stock traders have spent too much time in an artificial bubble. Peter Lynch's views are not out of date. In 2012, a financial idiot put the test to the test and suddenly managed to make $ 2 million in a problematic $ 20,000 trading period— anything but a cool trick.

According to the amateur investor, there have been clear trends in the spending patterns of women, young people, and low incomes. The man invested in stocks that anyone could own and noticed the trends before the bankers saw them and made significant profits.

How can you Track your Stock Portfolio?

If you decide to invest in stocks, creating an investment plan is the first step. However, once you've put your stock portfolio together, you're not ready. It is equally important to monitor your stock portfolio to see if it is still achieving your original goals. Some investors like to check the status of their investments daily. However, for many investors, this is not desirable or necessary. In other words, tracking your stock portfolio will depend on both the types of investments in your portfolio and the type of investor you are.

Monitor Shares

At a time when you have not invested in funds but individual stocks of your choosing, it is interesting to monitor them continuously. The most crucial goal here is to check whether a supply still meets the original criteria. In almost all cases, this depends heavily on the estimate of future expectations for the underlying company or on the stock market estimate. Many of these estimates are based on the company's earnings. You need to monitor changes that affect income.

Newspapers and Reports

Check financial news and announcements for your stock daily, weekly, or monthly. This includes new products, changes in management, or information about competitors. When analysts report on your actions, it is wise always to read them immediately as these can be of great importance to the market sentiment.

Online News Sources

Many brokers allow you to monitor your stock portfolio online. In some cases, there is also a direct link to news and relevant stock research. This way, not only can you see how your wallet is doing at a glance, but it also gives you an overview of the relevant news sources that can affect the price. Many brokers also offer the option to receive notifications via email or SMS when certain market developments occur. Does your broker not have this option? After that, you will get a large number of relevant news sources. You can get real-time information through both your brokerage and financial websites like Yahoo Finance, Morningstar, and Bloomberg. Since the stock market also reacts to developments in real-time, you can use this information to respond quickly to developments to maximize your returns.

Adjustments

So, you've put in a collar, and the prize instantly drops under your heading, bringing your bet in cash. And now? You imagined holding the position for at least a month, but here you have been in trading for less than a day and the prospect of hitting your maximum loss.

First, you need to assess whether your technical assumptions are still valid. Usually, when your technical analysis was perfect, there are some real events that you have overlooked. Does your stock depend on the bond market without your knowledge? Double-check your assumptions and check that your input logic is still valid. If not, eat the loss and move on. Calculate tuition fees to learn how to trade.

By the way, expect to do this often when you start. Trading is not an easy task, and this is why you should make as many mistakes in the simulation as you are showing off your strategies instead of jumping into a live account and sabotaging yourself.

Assuming your initial conclusions are still valid, this may be a temporary slowdown to shake weaker long traders. In these cases, you can try to restore your collar. First, sell your put position and determine which level is best for re-entering. If you sell your put, you will make money on that leg as if it had turned into cash. This is how you can benefit from the temporary downturn in the market.

When determining a secondary put level, consider the average risk. Remember, you are not selling your long position, so the average amount at risk per trade is still based on the initial put levels. The profit you make by selling the put will increase your account balance. Take this into account and determine a level that corresponds to your new risk per trade amount.

For example, if you make $ 450 selling the put, add it to your starting balance. Your new account balance is now x + 450, where x is the original account balance. Let's say your initial put level was 5 points, and your position size is ten stocks.

Given the increase in the account balance and the size of the existing position, what should the new put level look like so that the risk per trade remains similar? Well, that's simple arithmetic. Divide your new risk per transaction by the position size to find the stop loss or the distance from the put strike price.

Once the secondary put is in place, the next thing to consider is whether you want to leave the muted call in place. If you close this part of the trade, you will still make a profit as the call price would have decreased. Then you can hedge your position by repurchasing it at a lower price.

Execution

The first leg to be established is the long club leg. Like the covered call, it is an income generator that is entered with the thought that it will increase in value. The second stage is the married put. A married put is a put that covers your disadvantage. Think of this as a stop-loss order. Your maximum loss is limited to this level. The put is bought at an out-of-the-money price (which is below the current market level) at a price that corresponds to the maximum risk limit for that position. So, if you think you want to risk a move of only 5 points, the put will be bought at that price.

Finally, you need to write an out-of-the-money call just like you did with the covered market. Your long position covers this call. Make sure you execute your position in precisely this order so that the risk is minimized. Let's analyze the scenarios for this exchange.

If your stock falls in value, the underlying put will limit your maximum loss. Once the stock falls below the strike price of the put and then flows into the money, that leg will make a profit regardless of how low the stock price is. If you want to get out, you sell your stock, and you can sell your put, which would have increased in value.

Alternatively, if the stock gains value but does not reach the strike price of your call before maturity, you will earn the premium and the capital gain, but not the amount paid to buy the put. If the stock reaches the strike price of the call, this is the maximum possible profit on the share price, and you must sell your share at the strike price of the market.

In this case, you will again earn the capital gains on the long share segment and the premium on the covered call segment, but it will not be the premium paid to buy the put. There are also alternative scenarios.

Let's say the stock value is going down, but you're not sure that's a long-term thing. You feel like this is a passing bug, and it will show up soon. So, what are you doing? Should you leave all three positions? Well, this is where the decision to adjust your trade comes into play. You can reset the collar at different prices, i.e., change the strike prices of the call and put, or you can exit completely.

Technical and fundamental analysis should play a role in your decision. For now, remember that the collar is a wonderfully flexible strategy, and you can make money by making adjustments even if the trade is against you or if something unexpected happens. Now let's take a look at an example of a real number to see how it all works.

Fast trade execution

The Forex trading system allows you to get instant trade executions. You will not be exposed to delays, as is the case with options trading or other forms of market. Your order will be fulfilled at the best possible price instead of just guessing the price at which you should fulfill the order. The order of your choice will not merely slide, which can happen when trading options. In forex trading, the liquidity rate is much more essential to deal with the slippage that occurs when trading options.

Forex and Options

Forex trading, often referred to as forex trading or currency exchange, is a financial market where anyone can easily trade national currencies for specific amounts of profit. Perhaps some people believe that the US dollar will be more robust against the British pound or the euro. You can quickly come up with a strategy to influence this form of trading, and if your research turns out to be correct, you can make a lot of profits.

In the case of options trading, you buy and sell options on extensive futures, stocks, etc. You can invest by determining whether the price will rise or fall over a certain period. As with Forex trading, you can easily use your purchasing power, for example, to control a larger number of future stocks or shares that you might have in general. However, there are some differences between options trading and forex trading, which have been described below.

24-hour trading

One advantage you can get in forex trading over options trading is that you can trade 24 hours a day, five days a week, if you feel like it. The forex market is generally open longer than any other trading market. If your goal is to make double-digit profits in the market, having unlimited time each week to complete all of these trades is a great thing. Whenever any form of significant event occurs anywhere in the world, you can emerge as the first person to take full advantage of this situation in forex trading. You don't have to wait long for the market to open in the morning like it would in options trading. You can trade directly from your PC at any time of the day.

Liquid Funds

Forex trading generally has the added benefit of having more liquidity than any other trading market that includes options trading. There is no comparison of forex trading with an average daily market volume of around 2 trillion. The liquidity rate of forex trading can slightly exceed that of options trading. In simple terms, when it comes to trading, forex trades are filled very quickly compared to options trading. This also indicates a higher win rate. When you combine this with executing Forex trades instantly, you can start making more trades very quickly.

No commission

Forex or foreign exchange trading is generally free of any commission. This is mainly because, in forex trading, everything happens between banks, which also match buyers with potential sellers and are too fast. In short, in forex trading, the market is interbank. Hence, there is no evidence of brokerage or agent commission, as is the case with the other types of needs. There is a big difference between the asking price and the offer. This is where forex trading companies tend to get some of their profits. When trading options, you must pay brokerage fees, whether you want to buy or sell. Hence, trading the forex markets as compared to the options trading markets can save you a lot of money as there are no commissions.

More Leverage

In forex trading, you can get more leverage than in options trading. However, options trading also allows you to manage calls and use options in ways that significantly increase power. Influence can be significant when you know what a currency will do. In Forex trading, it is possible to reach 200: 1 or even more than in options trading, but it can also come close. So, it can be said that you can earn more with forex trading if the right move is made.

A minimum of Risk is Guaranteed

As forex traders must have position limits, the risk involved is also limited as the capabilities of the forex trading system can automatically initiate a margin call if the margin amount is much more considerable than that the account is worth in dollars. This helps forex traders not to lose so much if, by chance, their position tends to go the other way. It's a great security feature that isn't always available in other financial markets. How are options different from Forex in this respect? In the options aspect, you can only have a limited time to trade immediately before the options expire.

Stocks and Options

If you want to be a successful investor, you first need to understand the various investment opportunities properly. Most people allow their investment advisors to make decisions for them. Options and stocks are two of the most common investment markets when it comes to investment opportunities. Both are indeed traded similarly, but there is still a difference between the two. The share is a financing instrument. It shows ownership of a company and also helps identify a proper claim to company profits and assets. In simple terms, if you own the shares of a particular company, you own a portion of it that is proportional to the total number of shares that the company owns. For example, if you hold about 100 shares in a company that totals 1000 shares, you own 10% of that company.

As you already know, options are contracts to sell or buy an asset at a fixed price and within a set time. Unlike stocks, options contracts do not give you direct ownership of a company but rather the right to sell and buy a large number of company stocks.

Leveraged Profits

Options contract holders can take full advantage of the leverage of profits. For example, if the price of a stock increases by one percent, the cost of options is very likely to increase by ten percent. Therefore, it can be said that the profit of the options, in this case, is ten times higher than the share price.

Advantages of Trading Fundamental Analysis

Fundamental analysis is one of the ways to trade financial instruments, although not many are familiar with this analysis.

Understanding the trading process with this type of research can help you reduce the risk of loss with the basic versions.

At this point, we will list some of the benefits of trading fundamentals, including:

You will not trade too much on fundamental analysis as you will be online to trade when there is high impact news.

In fundamental analysis, there is a reason for every trade that allows you to make the right decisions.

The news causes high volatility in the market, which gives you a high probability of finding the right direction for your trade when the contract expires.

You prepare to trade because you know when the market will move.

The basics can help you get an idea of where the market is going through expert analysis.

The disadvantages of using fundamental analysis include:

It would help if you had a deep understanding of how the market reacts to fundamental news to trade options and make profits.

Messages can be very unpredictable and can move in any direction with minimal data modification.

It is difficult for a beginner to trade fundamentals.

You can go days without trading.

Prepare for Strangulation

A strangle is a trade in which you buy a call option and a put option at the same time. These are options on the same security with a similar fixed term but with a different fixed price. When you set up something called strangulation, your goal is to create an area or boundary around the current stock price. That way, you hope the stock price will move beyond the limit. In that case, buy both options. So, the real risk is the total cost of buying both options.

Let's say the stock price is between $ 98 and $ 100. You could set up a strangle by buying a call option with an exercise price of $ 105 and a put option with an exercise price of $ 95. If the stock price stayed between $ 95 and $ 105, you would lose money trading. There would be a maximum loss if you went to maturity and kept the same strategy. You could reduce your losses by selling the position early if you could find a buyer.

The maximum gain on the positive side of strangulation is theoretically unlimited. If the market value stays above the set price used to buy a call option in the trade, plus the cost of the call option, you make a profit. And if in principle, it continues to exceed the strike price, you will make more profit. Your yield will be reduced by the total cost of purchasing the two options.

Conversely, you will make a profit on a put if the market value falls below the set price minus the price paid for it. This would be the break-even price for the put option.

If there is a massive price movement after the profit call, this type of setup ensures that profits are made regardless of which direction the stock moves. The key to building trade is choosing the right strike prices. The more significant the difference between the exercise prices, the lower the total cost of entering the business. However, there is a smaller chance of winning because a more extensive price range means the stock must

move a greater distance before realizing—
profits from trading.

Straddles

A straddle is a variation of Strangles trading. In this case, you buy a call option and a put option at the same time. They also apply to the same inventory and have the same expiration date. The difference between a straddle and a strangle is that they have the same strike prices. A straddle limits the range of trade. Because they have the same strike price, you increase your chances of the stock moving in a way that will help you make more significant profits.

Let's take two examples. For the first example, we will set up an astraddle. This will be hypothetical, but we'll start with current Apple pricing as an example and use strike prices of $ 240 for calls and puts. Fourteen days before expiration, a call option with an exercise price of $ 240 costs $ 6.20, and a put option costs $ 6.17. So, the total investment required to open the position would be $ 1,237. For example, suppose the earnings demand is ten days before maturity, and the stock price increases by $ 20 per share. The put option drops to $ 0.43 or $ 43. The call option goes up to $ 20.45, so we can sell the call option for $ 2.045. We could also sell the put option to get rid of it and get the $ 43 back. So, our net profit would be $ 43 + $ 2045 - $ 1237 = $ 851.

On the other hand, if the stock price fell by $ 20 in the event of a bad call on earnings, the put option would increase to $ 20.28 while the call option would decrease to $ 0.30. So, we see that it would produce similar results regardless of which direction the stock price should move.

Now consider a choke with a $ 240 call option and a $ 235 put option. In this case, buying the put option would cost $ 393, while the call option would cost $ 6.20. So, the total investment would be $ 1,013. So, it's a little cheaper to set up Strangle. The results are the same at the top. If the price rises to $ 260 per share, the call option will generate the same profit as before, but the put option will drop to $ 17. We could just let it expire worthlessly or try to resell it for $ 17 back. The Strangle would be bearish if the stock did not fall further as we chose a lower strike price. If it drops to $ 220, the put option would be worth $ 15.67. So, our profit would be $ 1,567 - $ 1,013 + $ 30 = $ 584 assuming we could sell the call option for $ 30.

Always have an Exit Plan

Picking a stock, formulating an option strategy to generate income from the stock's performance, and then contacting your broker about initiating an opening deal is an excellent place to start. However, this plan is not a complete strategy. The most important part of an option strategy is not entering but exiting.

Profit from an option strategy may result from buying the underlying security at a price below market value, accepting a cash settlement for a declining stock option, or even from profit increasing the cost of the option premium by selling the contract before maturity.

However, they believe that the asset you have identified may allow you to develop a profitable strategy for trading options. Guesswork and hopes should not be part of this strategy. Before entering into any opening transaction, make sure you are clear about your specific goal for signing the contract. After completing the opening deal, you will be presented with one of three possible outcomes:

- The market and the target stocks have moved in the direction you expected.

- The target market or stocks are moving in an unexpected direction, resulting in unforeseen losses.

- The target market or stock is moving in an unexpected direction, resulting in unforeseen profits.

Similarly, you should have three ready-made answers for each of these developments:

- When you are faced with the first result, you should already have an exit strategy in place. Whatever is happening around you, as long as your resources are on the right track, don't deviate from your plan.

- If there are unexpected changes that are unfavorable to your position on the underlying asset, what plan have you made to terminate the contract so that you can minimize your losses?

- What plan have you put in place to exit the contract if you have made unforeseen favorable changes in your position about the underlying asset so that you can take advantage of these gains?

Make sure you can answer all three questions before entering into an option contract. Once you've laid the groundwork for successful options trading, stick to your plan even if you think you can make a few extra dollars by improvising.

Adapt your Strategy to Market Situations

Once you enter the world of professional options trading, you will gain confidence when you see your efforts pay off in getting your options to account back. When you move from a level 1 trading account to a level 2 trading account, you will likely develop a preference for a specific type of options trading, possibly hedged calls or married puts. Familiarity with the language and mechanics of the options trading profession is something that will work in your favor. However, it is essential to remember that as you level up, you will have access to a broader range of trading tools and strategies.

As you gain knowledge and experience, keep in mind that no matter how well you are familiar with a select number of options trading strategies, there are always additional nuances that can improve your skills as a trader and increase the profitability of your endeavors. The key to success is not just choosing the best strategy in terms of the performance of the underlying asset. It is also necessary to consider general market conditions and assess whether such conditions could affect the future performance of that asset. Although a strategy may have worked under similar circumstances in the past, you can tweak your design taking into account changes in current conditions to ensure that you continue to build on your previous success.

What every Investor should Avoid
Double up to cover losses

The "doubling down" is an excellent example of how an options trader can ignore his original exit strategy if the underlying market or stock is not behaving as he expected it to when he initially developed his system.

For example, suppose a trader buys a call option for 100 shares of Company B with an exercise price of $ 45. At the time the call option was purchased, Company B was trading at $ 44. The trader expects the stock price to rise to $ 47 before the contract expires. However, immediately after the opening transaction, the share price falls to $ 43.

The premium for a call option with a strike price of $ 45 is now further out of the money than when it was opened. Also, it will take a long time for the deadline to expire. Therefore, to offset potential losses if the stock climbs to just $ 46, the trader may be tempted to "double" by buying another $ 45 call option at the reduced premium price.

If this trader had just bought stocks, he could have celebrated the stock's unexpected decline in value and immediately bought as many additional stocks as possible with the goal of higher long-term returns. Options trading works differently, however. The options trader focuses on short term returns. If the stock price does not cash the contract by the expiration date, the trader will lose not just one deal but two.

The smart trader will remember that they made an exit plan for this scenario and stick to it. While it may be tempting to buy an additional call option, it should judge the wisdom of that purchase by wondering if it would buy the second call option if it weren't already in the middle of a trade. If this isn't usually a contract he would have made - and it is not, because that was not his strategy in his opening deal - then contrary-to-expect market conditions and stock performance are likely the worst reasons for him to change that view.

Instead, he should stay on his contract to see if the stock eventually recovers and makes the deal profitable, or sell the contract right away, reduce his losses and look for another opportunity that makes more sense.

Apply the Rules

As an options trader, you compete with other traders and investors. Much of the success of your investment, including making valuable connections in the investment world, comes from your ability to follow the rules. The stock market is a living thing, and the activity of traders has a significant impact on their health and volatility. We are all tempted to be lonely, leaving a legacy of innovation, but understanding the basics will work in your favor.

In particular, option prices rise or fall due to changes in stock prices and volatility.

So, when stock prices rise, call options to make money and put options, lose money. When stock prices go down, put options, make money, and call options to lose money. Options also move in terms of volatility; When stock prices are stable, greater volatility can drive option prices up. So, when volatility increases, buying options make money. When volatility subsides, selling options make money.

CONCLUSION

The last time you prepared your company's financial statements, filed taxes, or reviewed your investment portfolio, you may have included "cash and cash equivalents" as part of the calculation of your total assets. Your cash assets are assets such as cars and trucks, office equipment, or real estate that can be quickly converted into cash via the sale. Assets of value may not be considered liquid unless you can sell them quickly for cash. Selling goods for cash fast requires a market, whether it's a garage sale, auction, or media advertisement. However, it also requires enough potential buyers so that you don't have to wait for the right buyer to come and pay you the asking price. The greater the number of buyers, the greater the competition, and the greater the opportunities to make a sale, the greater the liquidity of the asset. Of course, when you sell an obscure or unique item, regardless of its value, it is inherently less liquid.

Liquidity in options trading is similar. For a stock to be considered liquid, it would have to trade at 1,000,000 shares per day. Most blue-chip stocks, such as Microsoft or General Electric, are liquid stocks. Smaller, lesser-known companies may not only trade in lower volumes. They didn't trade once a day. Such stores are considered illiquid.

Illiquid options contracts, such as assets and stocks, have a relatively small market of buyers and sellers competing to buy and sell them. All stock traders buy and sell the same store for a particular company. At the same time, a single action can lead to countless option contracts, each with different strike prices and expiration dates. As a result, options become more illiquid than stocks.

Additionally, the size of the market for a given option contract can range from illiquid to liquid, even though the security itself is generally considered to be liquid security. A stock is deemed to be illiquid if it trades fewer than 1,000,000 shares per day. Similarly, you should consider an illiquid option if it has an open interest of fewer than 50 times the number of contracts you will trade. For example, if you are selling five options contracts on Company XYZ, that company should have an open interest in options transactions of at least 250 deals.

The main reasons for avoiding illiquid options markets are cost and return on investment. Whenever you complete an opening transaction, there is a buyer and a seller of a contract. This contract has an ask price (the amount an investor is willing to pay for the deal) and a bid price (the amount an investor is ready to sell the contract for). But the real value of the contract.

COPYRIGHTS

©Copyright 2020 by William Earn

All rights reserved

This book:

"OPTIONS TRADING CRASH COURSE 2021 volume 3: The Best Guide for Beginners of The Market Psychology to Use the Right Strategies and Avoid the Commons Mistakes to Create Your Passive Income for a Living. "

Written By

William Earn

This document aims to provide precise and reliable details on this subject and the problem under discussion.

The product is marketed on the assumption that no officially approved bookkeeping or publishing house provides other available funds.

Where a legal or qualified guide is required, a person must have the right to participate in the field.

A statement of principle, which is a subcommittee of the American Bar Association, a committee of publishers, and is approved. A copy, reproduction, or distribution of parts of this text, in electronic or written form, is not permitted.

The recording of this document is strictly prohibited. Any retention of this text is only with the written permission of the publisher and all liberties authorized.

The information provided here is correct and reliable, as any lack of attention or other means resulting from the misuse or use of the procedures or instructions contained therein is the total and absolute obligation of the user addressed.

The author is not obliged, directly or indirectly, to assume civil liability for any restoration, damage, or loss resulting from the data collected here. The respective authors retain all copyrights not kept by the publisher.

The information contained herein is solely and universally available for information purposes. The data is presented without a warranty or promise of any kind.

The trademarks used are without approval, and the patent is issued without the trademark owner's permission or protection.

The logos and labels in this book are the property of the owners themselves and are not associated with this text.

CPSIA information can be obtained
at www.ICGtesting.com
Printed in the USA
BVHW081724060421
604346BV00011B/208